For Sahoko

# IRELAND

## PHOTOGRAPHY LIAM BLAKE

## TEXT DAVID PRITCHARD

**Published in Ireland by Real Ireland Design Limited**

First published in 1998 by **Real Ireland Design Limited** ©.
27 Beechwood Close, Boghall Road, Bray, Co. Wicklow, Ireland.
Telephone: (01) 2860799. Fax: (01) 2829962.

Photography Liam Blake ©.
Text David Pritchard.
Book & jacket design Brian Murphy.

**Printed in Ireland**

British Library Cataloguing in Publication Data.
A catalogue record for this book is available from the British
Library

ISBN 0946887446

# INTRODUCTION

The name Ireland offers an insight into the place itself and its people. It is a derivation of the ancient Irish word Eire, which probably means western. To its own people, then, Ireland was the country in the west, the last island before the vast Atlantic ocean. The Greeks and Romans transliterated the same word into Ierne, or Ivernia, eventually calling the island Hibernia - the land of winter. This perhaps reflects one European view of Ireland, a cold wet remote island lost off the western edge of the world. Yet Ireland's isolation is illusory, for there has been a constant human interchange between her shores and those of her eastern neighbours for millennia. On this level the culture of the island has been woven into an unique cultural tapestry through the mingling of the diverse peoples who have contributed to its genius.

This book seeks to explore these seemingly contradictory visions of Ireland - as Geographical dead-end or human crossroads. The first part charts the movement of the nameless folk who made their mark upon the landscape in Prehistory and at length emerged as the 'Irish', a distinct and recognizable People. The second looks at those remote western and northern coasts which face the wild ocean, the grandiose rim of the known world before the discovery of America and the cradle and death bed of a Gaelic speaking society whose roots were found in the Stone Age. The last section covers the east of Ireland and Dublin, the gateway through which Viking, Norman and British colonists have influenced the historical evolution of the Irish over the last 1000 years.

Liam Blake's photographs offer an unsurpassed visual record of the beauties of Ireland and the day to day life of her people. His work over the years for the Real Ireland range of postcards has been a significant artistic achievement, influencing the perception of Ireland by public and other photographers alike. His images in this book cover a wide spectrum of the Irish experience, ranging from small details of everyday life to sweeping panoramic landscapes. His vision and understanding of the Irish landscape and people provide the driving force for this book.

# THE LEGACY OF ANCIENT IRELAND

The land of Ireland - earth, rock and green mantle - has been a remarkable cradle to her people. That such a small island could produce so many exceptional scholars and writers seems unbelievable, especially when it seems a geographical backwater on the furthest edge of Europe. One of the most important facets of the psyche of the Irish must be the love they bear for their damp little country. 'Mother Ireland' may be an anachronistic expression today - a left over from the inward looking Catholic attitudes of the de Valera era. Nevertheless, the concept expresses an age old love for the land itself, which is invariably perceived as a feminine presence. Mountains such as the Paps - in mythology the breasts of the Goddess Aºne - in South Kerry and the Three Sisters of the Dingle Peninsula reflect the longlasting old perception of the land of Ireland as a woman.

Since the arrival of the first farmers on the shores of Ireland nearly 7,000 years ago, the soil of Ireland has been sacred, a living organism which held the secrets of life and fertility. To the monk Blathmac - writing in the 8th. century -

the very trees of Ireland bled on the day that Christ was crucified,
'There was blood on the breasts of the world in the heights of every great forest.'

This belief in the feminine power of the land has persisted throughout Irish history. The Celtic fertility goddesses of ancient Ireland survive today as the females saints of Pattern and Holy Well, whilst the four great annual pagan holidays have been Christianized into festivals like Halloween. Just as the basic settlement patterns of rural Ireland were established in prehistoric times, so were many of the underlying traditions and attitudes of its people. By the early Christian period - when monasteries and Viking ports were established as the first large urban settlements - Ireland had been an agricultural and pastoral society for the best part of 6,000 years. This prehistoric legacy - the marriage of the Irish people to the earth - is still relevant, even in the age of television and the motor car.

The attachment of the Irish to their land is a continuing thread, which runs through Irish history and binds the past to the present. In 1948 an old Clare farmer - talking about local beliefs con-

The Three Sisters mountains and mount Brandon, Co Kerry.

cerning fate and destiny - described an ancient tradition which encapsulates the symbolic relationship of man and the earth beneath his feet.

'I wish to mention the belief the old people had that it was laid out for a person, from the time the crown of his head came into the world, where his place of death was. For this person it was laid out that for him, or for her, the side of the road would be as a sod of death, for another the middle of the road, or out on the brown mountains, or in the loneliness of the wood or - as God save us from danger - a person could have as a sod of death a violent death.'

The legend of the three sods - of birth, death and burial - may well be traceable back to the religious ideas of the Stone Age farmers, who carefully covered their passage graves with alternating layers of stone and cut sods of earth. Yet nobody would suggest that the people of West Clare in 1948 were anything but strictly

Creevykeel Court Tomb, Co. Sligo.

orthodox Catholics. However, their beliefs and ideas were the sum of changing influences over thousands of years, a complex mixture of new and old which set the boundaries of their character. This may be compared to the landscape of Ireland, whose natural face has equally been changed by the arrival of each wave of settlers and colonists.

Ireland may seem insignificant when seen on a world map, but within her confines there is a surprising variety of landscape. The natural beauty of the island has been much modified by the interaction of man with the environment and features which seem the result of natural growth or climactic change are also at least in part the result of human activity. During the 10,000 years or since the first hunter gatherers crossed over to Ireland from Scotland, the appearance and dominant flora of the landscape have changed repeatedly. This process is ongoing. The wild fuchsia and rhododendron which grow so profusely in Irish

Standing stone, Punchestown, Co. Kildare.

hedgerows and through deciduos forests like those around Killarney, were introduced only 150 years or so ago, whilst such exotic domestic animals as llamas, sika deer and ostriches have made their appearance within the last decade. A rich growth of planted woodland now covers valleys like Glendalough which in 19th. century paintings are bare of trees. Vast plantations of pine trees have utterly changed the appearance of uplands which in living memory were bogs or heathery wastes.

The introduction of farming into Ireland around 6,500 years ago stands as perhaps the single greatest leap forward in her history. The first agriculturists arrived on the north coasts and gradually moved south and westwards until large areas of the country were under cultivation or tillage. Generally they avoided the marshy lowlands and kept to the wooded hills, hacking out clearings for their herds and crops by the slash and burn method, then moving on when the soil was exhausted. Within a few centuries

Newgrange, Co. Meath.

communities of farmers began to establish themselves in northern and western areas, building themselves houses and erecting stone wall enclosures for their herds. Today many of these field systems have been covered by peat bog, as at the Ceide fields in County Mayo, where 4,500 year old stone walls have been uncovered by archaeologists.

It seems that by the end of the Neolithic around 4,000 years ago, the basic pattern of Irish farming until modern times had already been laid down. As it is today, the main emphasis was on beef and dairy farming - although the animals were oxen rather than cattle - with pigs, goats and sheep also common domestic animals. Cereal crops were not as important and much less ground was given over to their production. It is also likely that in some regions social organization had progressed beyond the family group to larger tribal units or even rudimentary kingdoms ruled by priest-kings, although it is unlikely that the scattered

Stone detail, Newgrange, Co. Meath.

Poulnabrone Dolmen, the Burren, Co. Clare.

inhabitants of the island shared any sense of a common identity.

The visible monuments of Neolithic age in Ireland are the stone tombs built by these early farmers. Examples of the most common early types, the 'court' grave and the 'passage' grave, may be seen in many counties in the northern half of Ireland. There are distinct differences between these two forms of tombs which suggest that they reflect either separate waves of immigrants or differ-ing social structures. Court graves are usually found in isolation, sometimes near to - or even built over - a prehis-toric farmhouse. There is a fine court grave in the Ceide fields system for example, which undoubtedly served the people who built the adjacent houses and stone walls. In court graves a circu-lar or semi-circular area is recessed in front of a long stone walled chamber, which has been covered by a mound of earth or stone. Their elongated shape and structure has affinities with the long

Beehive hut, Slea Head, Co. Kerry.

barrows of England, suggesting they are an Irish version developed by settlers who probably arrived via southern Scotland. It seems likely that court graves were generally the communal burial place of a single family and its descendants in the immediate vicinity, a prehistoric version of the family plots that are still found in country graveyards.

Passage graves, on the other hand, pose a number of questions. They belong to a category of prehistoric tomb found along the Atlantic coasts of Europe, where a passage leads into a chamber in which the bones or ashes of the dead are stored, the whole structure concealed beneath a circular mound held in place by curb stones. Although a number of passage graves stand alone, most are found in clusters, often on high places which are visible for miles around. This suggests that they formed ritual centres for quite large districts, a view supported by the magnificent tombs in the Boyne Valley of Meath.

The passage graves at Knowth, Newgrange and Dowth rank amongst the finest prehistoric monuments in the world. The huge restored mound of New Grange, almost flying saucer-like on its ridge beside the river Boyne, is justly one of the great tourist sites of Ireland. The triple spiral motif associated with New Grange has come to symbolize this huge achievement of Neolithic technology. Whilst single and double spirals are common motifs in Stone Age art, the triple spiral only occurs at this site, where it is carved on the entrance stone and inside the chamber of the passage grave. Although its exact meaning is a mystery, some scholars believe the triple spiral symbolizes the cycle of birth, life and death.

It is tempting to see Newgrange and Knowth as 'royal' tombs, built for the rulers of a primitive kingdom based on the Meath region. If this is so, then it marks an early step in the evolution of isolated farming communities into the 'kingdoms' into which Ireland was divided from the dawn of its recorded history up to the end of the 16th. century.

Regardless of the truth of this theory, the long period between the building of the Brug na Boyne passage graves and the arrival of the Celts saw many cultural innovations and increased links with prehistoric societies in Britain and the continent of Europe. Towards the end of the Neolithic age two new types of megalithic - or large stone - tomb became popu-

Sunset, Blasket islands, Co. Kerry.

Clonmacnoise, Co. Offaly.

Round tower, Glendalough, Co. Wicklow.

lar. The portal-tomb or dolmen, found mainly in the northwest of Ireland (although there are some fine examples in Leinster and around Galway Bay) seems to have been a simplified local variation of the court grave. The gallery grave, on the other hand, occurs mainly in the south and west of Ireland and may have been developed by migrants arriving into Munster from western France.

The beginning of the Bronze Age, around 2000 B.C., brought Ireland into a trading network that already existed throughout Europe. Substantial deposits of copper and gold made the island attractive to miners and metalworkers, encouraging a new wave of settlers. Stone circles, perhaps the most enchanting of all Irish prehistoric monuments, probably date from this period. Little is known about the purpose of these mysterious sites, although archaeological evidence suggests they had some ritual significance and were often aligned to the sunrise and sunset. Considered with the large

St. Kevin's church, Glendalough, Co. Wicklow.

number of single standing stones and alignments that abound in many parts of Ireland, they suggest the expansion of an increasing population into areas that were previously thinly populated.

From around 1200 B.C. onwards it appears that Ireland experienced a fresh wave of settlement, brought about by the expansion of peoples speaking 'Indo-European' - the language which is the ancestor of almost all modern European languages and Sanskrit and Hindi in India. During the 'Dowris Period' around 700 B.C., much of the island seems to have been controlled by a rich aristocratic class, who made exquisite weapons and possessed expensive imported luxuries like amber and jet necklaces.

By and large, however, Ireland was a pastoral society, where wealth was interpreted by the number of cattle a man owned. The Celts of the La Téne culture, who are believed to have began arriving around 500 B.C., found themselves in a society

Near Cloghane, Dingle peninsula, Co. Kerry.

The Fastnet lighthouse, West Cork.

that was not very dissimilar to those they knew in Britain and in Western Europe. Despite their divisions, it is not unreasonable to suspect that the people on the island by now shared some sense of Irishness which transcended tribe or clan and included all those living within the confines of its shores. The Celts themselves came as invaders or mercenaries, relying on the quality of the iron weapons they carried to impose their authority on the natives of the island. Iron working certainly arrived in Ireland at the same time as the earliest La Téne artifacts discovered by archaeologists, suggesting it was a Celtic introduction.

The spread of 'Celtic' culture and language probably occurred over a number of centuries and involved several waves of immigrants, some from Britain, some from France and Belgium and - according to legend at least - some from northern Spain. Earlier peoples already present were assimilated and lost their identities in new kingdoms and power

Eyeries village, Beara, Co. Cork.

The Great Blasket islands from Dunmore Head, Co. Kerry.

Taking the sheep to higher pasture, Dingle, Co. Kerry.

groupings. Sites like Navan Fort and Tara - which were already important tribal centres - were taken over to become the capitals of quite large dynastic kingdoms. On the treeless western seaboard dry walled promontory forts and circular cashels became common defences. Two types of lesser domestic dwellings came to the fore for lesser landowners. The crannçg - an artificial island built on a lake - had roots in the Bronze Age. It became very common in the Iron Age, surviving as a type until as late as 1600.

The ring fort, a house within an palisaded circular bank of earth, seems to have evolved in the early centuries of the Christian era. Ring forts - which had the same function as a modern farmhouse and its yard - are the most common prehistoric monuments in Ireland, seen in large numbers throughout the countryside.

The most important single contribution made by the dying society of Roman Britain to Ireland was the Christian reli-

The Ring of Beara, West Cork.

gion. Christianity was well established in England by A.D.400 and had almost certainly been brought to Ireland by individual migrant workers and soldiers returning home. It seems likely that by A.D.431 there were sizeable Christian communities in some parts of Ireland, since in that year Germanus of Auxerre, who was trying to purge pelagian heretics from the English Church, appointed one Palladius to be 'the first deacon of the Irish Christians'.

According to tradition there were other bishops active in Ireland at this time - including figures like Declan of Ardmore (Waterford) and Ibarus of Begerin (Wexford) who were active in the area of southeast Ireland opposite the Welsh coast. Yet the work of these missionaries has been overshadowed by the legend of one man - Patrick, the patron saint of Ireland. It seems that Patrick was a Briton from the north-west part of

Ballydonegan, Beara, West Cork.

View over Bantry bay, Co. Cork.

Italian gardens, Glengarriff, Co. Cork.

Green fields near Dursey island, West Cork.

England and the story of his slavery in Ireland as a child is quite likely the truth - although the same story of the slave converting his former masters is told of the founder of the Ethiopian church. He may have begun his mission in Ireland ministering to a community of Christians established in the north east of Ireland from Galloway in Scotland. This theory is certainly supported by his associations with Armagh and Downpatrick in southern Ulster.

However, his avowed purpose was the conversion of the pagan Irish. From his base in Armagh he appears to have undertaken extensive missionary journeys, travelling to areas like Mayo and Donegal that were still entirely heathen. In his autobiographical 'Confessio' Patrick states that he had personally converted thousands of the Irish, a testament to both his persuasive powers and stamina. The association of his name

Ross castle, Kilarney, Co. Kerry.

with places like Croagh Patrick and Lough Derg - which were likely sites of pagan worship - might be apocryphal. Nevertheless it suggests he had an important role in converting the north-western counties. However, other legends, for instance his activities at Tara (Meath), are probably fabrications. Most likely they were invented for propaganda purposes by later Kings of Ulster who wished to bolster the paramountcy in Ireland of Patrick's church at Armagh.

The conversion of Ireland was undoubtedly a longer and more complex process than the legend of Patrick allows. One of its notable features of Irish Christianity was the incorporation of Celtic gods and festivals into its fabric. The most famous example is Brigid of Kildare, cited as one of the founders of the Irish church in Leinster. Brigid was the most important Celtic fertility goddess, worshipped not only in Ireland but across Europe in the pagan era.

Sunset, lakes of Killarney, Co. Kerry.

Muckross gardens, Killarney, Co. Kerry.

Muckross house, Killarney, Co. Kerry.

The Christian saint's day - February 1-was shared with the pagan feast of Imbolc, the first of the four great annual holidays. The perpetually lit sacred fire at the church and shrine of Brigid in Kildare was the continuation of a heathen practice at a holy place that was probably a pagan temple before it was Christianized.

If the Christianity of the people was tinged with a pagan element, the organization of the early Irish church developed along more orthodox lines. The monastic community rapidly became the heart of Irish Christianity, the centre from which radiated the missionary impulse and scholarly wisdom for which Ireland was noted in the Dark Ages. The earliest monasteries were small and quite austere, intended for those who wished to live removed from other men. They may be typified by remote little island settlements like Skellig Michael off the Kerry coast, which comprised only a simple church and a few beehive huts.

Near Glenbeigh, Ring of Kerry.

Later monasteries, however, were more ambitious and sometimes grew to become like small towns, with abbots as powerful as kings and large populations of monks and lay servants. Many of the great monasteries of the midlands, for example Clonmacnoise (Offaly), opened up huge new areas which had been thinly inhabited and cleared rough expanses of forest and marsh for cultivation and pasturage.

The monasteries of Ireland were not communal in organization like those of the Benedictines and mainland European orders. They consisted of a number of individuals who carried out their religious observances in private, assembling only for church services and to help administer the monastery. Nevertheless, large foundations like Glendalough (Wicklow) had a number of important social and religious functions. Despite its seeming remoteness, this monastery stands at the hub of a network of roads which cross the Wicklow

Market day, Kilorglin, Co. Kerry.

mountains from east to west and north to south. By the 10th. century a large walled settlement had grown up at the mouth of the valley where St. Kevin had established himself as a hermit. Glendalough, with its round tower, churches and crosses, attracted many pilgrims to visit the sites associated with its patron saint and was also a market and trade centre for the region. Yet in addition to the main church and shrine of St. Kevin, smaller monastic enclosures in the valley were provided for monks who wished to live in isolation.

The Irish monasteries of the early Christian era became famous for their scholarship and illuminated manuscripts like the Book of Kells. With their flowering and the journeys of missionary Irish monks to Britain and the Continent of Europe, the long prehistory of Ireland finally drew to a close and the island slowly emerged on the stage of recorded history.

The Cliffs of Moher, Co. Clare.

Detail, the Burren, Co. Clare.

## THE WEST OF IRELAND AND THE ATLANTIC COAST.

The winds that blow so frequently over Ireland have played a major part in shaping both the landscape and history of the island. They are a constant factor in the climate and there are few days in the year when the air is still. Savage autumn gales from the Atlantic, icy gusts crossing Europe from Siberia and warm African breezes originating in the Sahara end up on the Irish shores. These never ending pattern of winds cause the changes in light which make the landscape hazy and muted on one day and bright and clear on another.

Ireland, particularly in its western regions, is a land of horizons made glorious by towering, cloudy skies. The artist Paul Henry captures this aspect brilliantly in his landscape paintings, placing huddled cottages against dark hills and mountains dwarfed by huge skies. More than anything else, perhaps, the rela-

Collecting water, near Kilfinora, Co. Clare.

Rock concert, Lisdoonvarna, Co. Clare.

tionship between the western coasts and the world is defined by the vast emptiness that stretches to the western horizon from the cliffs where the land abruptly meets the wild Atlantic seas.

The unique western Irish landscape must be amongst the most beautiful in the world. Since man first arrived on these coasts great forests of oak and elm have disappeared from the slopes of the mountains and blanket bogs have

formed a shroud over arable lands that once held the settlements of Neolithic pastoralists. Yet the bones of the land remain the same and high peaks still rise from the western edge of Ireland to break the flatness of her central plain.

Like all human beings the Irish have given a central role to mountains in their mythology as the homes of the Gods. Yet the nearness of the low Irish peaks gives an uncommon intimacy between

Aftrer Mass, Inisheer, Aran islands.

Music and the craic, Galway city.

the deities of the high places and their worshippers below. Mount Brandon, the second highest mountain in Ireland barely exceeds 3000 feet in height and can be climbed in a few hours from the Dingle peninsula beneath. On its windy mist covered summit is one of the great holy places in Ireland, dedicated to the shadowy figure of Brendan the Navigator, a 7th. century abbot whose legend blends memories of real voyages by early Christian monks with Celtic myths about

the western Isles of the Dead

The annual pilgrimage to the oratory and crumbling well on top of Mount Brandon is undoubtedly extremely ancient in origin, quite likely as old as the habitation of man on the Dingle peninsula itself. But the appeal of the peak is far greater than its historical associations. On the rare occasions the mists clear the summit offers a bird's eye view of the west of Ireland, laying out the loneliness of the

River Corrib, Galway city.

mountainous coastline against the vast and frightening expanses of the Atlantic ocean. This view encapsulates a basic truth about Ireland, that for millennia it stood on the rim of the known world, between Europe on one hand and the ocean - which divides all men from the unattainable realms of the spirit - on the other.

The western isolation of the Atlantic coasts of Ireland have made them the last cultural outpost of the European continent. Until modern times the traditional life style of its fishermen and pastoralists in many ways remained prehistoric, with archaic practices such as rundale farming (the communal sharing of fields) and transhumance (moving animals to upland summer pastures) is still common. The traditional western cottage - the long-house - is derived from primitive thatch and stone dwellings that had changed little from Stone Age types, whilst corbelled stone huts were still being built for use as outhouses until

Traditional cottage, Connemara.

View of the Twelve Bens mountains, Connemara.

Morning mist, Derryclare lough, Connemara.

Ballynahinch lake, Connemara.

Aaesleigh waterfall, Co. Mayo.

recent decades. Human beings have lived on these coasts for a very long time, moving into the region from the east, south and north.

The towns and villages of the West are for the most part comparatively small and rarely more than a few hundred years old. The exceptions are ports like Limerick, Galway and Sligo and Anglo-Norman towns such as Askeaton (Limerick) and Athenry (Galway), estab-lished on the Shannon estuary or the western margins of the central plains. In the Middle Ages these cities and walled burghs were on the western frontier of Feudal Europe, isolated islands of urban civilization in a hinterland dominated by 'wild' Irish and degenerate Norman chieftains. Little enough remains of their Medieval heritage and today Georgian and Victorian buildings domi-nate the streets of town and city alike in the West.

Killary harbour, Co. Mayo.

Clifden town, Connemara.

Yet, despite the charming ambience of the quaint West Cork villages or small towns of north Donegal, they are dwarfed by the wild landscape in which they are set. Even the spires and slate roofs of sizable settlement like Dingle (Kerry) or Clifden (Galway) seem toylike afterthoughts set against towering mountains and wild skies. Perhaps no earthbound human eye can catch the essential unity of the Atlantic coasts. From south to north, range upon range of stark mountains are separated by stony wastes or patchy human cultivation. Perhaps only from the skies above would it be possible to comprehend the essential unity of these wild shores, bounded between rocky hills and bogland on one side and the endless reaches of the ocean on the other.

To a migratory bird, blown by fierce winds over the empty Atlantic from Africa or the Americas, the south western margins of Ireland might first appear as a distant speck on the horizon - a shad-

Hay fields, Achill island, Co. Mayo.

Clew bay and Croagh Patrick mountain, Co. Mayo.

Pilgrims, Croagh Patrick mountain, Co. Mayo.

owy hint that the ocean was about to meet land again. Eventually this hazy smudge on the infinite grey of the sea materializes into a rocky coast where the sea carves deep inlets between mountainous peninsulas. Scattered islands, sprinkled a few miles offshore, mark the tentative western limits of the land of Ireland. From the air they seem insignificant, these tiny specks of rock and soil against the bulk of the mainland, yet in a very real sense they stand as the westernmost boundary of human habitation in Europe. Some - like Skellig Michael off the coast of Kerry - seem almost uninhabitable, yet are spotted with the ruined churches and beehive huts of reclusive Irish monks who lived there a thousand years ago. On others, such as the Blaskets off the Dingle peninsula, the slowly disintegrating cottages of populations who left within living memory bear mute witness to the difficulties of sustaining life in so isolated and impoverished an environment.

Carrowmore, Co. Sligo.

Fishermen, Glencar lake, Co. Leitrim.

Yet a number of these small islands are still inhabited and form some of the remotest communities in Europe, often completely cut off for days at a time in stormy weather. The Aran islands, off Galway Bay further north, typify the cultural depth of these ancient societies and their archaic traditions and life styles. Clusters of long-house cottages and tiny stone fields hark back to a type of farming that in prehistoric times was the norm throughout much of Europe. Gaelic, the language of the people who dwell on the islands, is the oldest north of the Alps. Despite their remoteness, the Aran Islands have had a profound influence on the mainstream of Irish cultural life during its most vital era in the early 1900's, providing inspiration to the writer John Synge and artists like Jack Yeats and Paul Henry.

The coasts off which these islands lie are beautiful but forbidding, harsh expanses of bare rock and rough grass, with few trees larger than a gnarled, wind twisted

Benbulben mountain, Co. Sligo.

thorns or hazel scrub. Ireland - as every Irish school child knows - is shaped like a sitting bear, with its back to Britain and its upper and lower legs facing west. The lower legs, comprising the mountainous sandstone promontories of West Cork and Kerry, are deeply indented by the sea and bordered for the most part by cliffs and stony islets. These barren coasts have little to offer man, but in summer serve as the breeding ground for thousands of seabirds. Cormorants, Shags, Razorbills, Guillemots and Kittiwake cram onto the ledges, whilst Puffins and Gannets nest on the rocky islands and headlands. Gull colonies add to the general noise and air of excitement, leaving ocean-wandering Manx Shearwaters and Storm Petrels to seek the peace of the remotest islands and rocks to make their annual breeding visit ashore. Their departure heralds the coming of winter, when the near deserted cliffs are buffeted by ferocious gales and rain storms.

Malin head, Co. Donegal.

Inland from the cliffs rises a wall of mountains, broken by valleys and coastal strips where fields, farmhouses and the occasional small town or hamlet mark the presence of man on the landscape. In the extreme southwest the hilly and rich Cork countryside peters out in the narrow Mizen and Durrus peninsulas, with their distinctive two dormer one and a half storey farmhouses. Further north, beyond Bantry with its imposing mansion on the hill above the town, the country becomes more rugged. The lush vegetation of Glengarriff - with the gardens of Garinish Island like an emerald in the bay- is a green splash against the desolate mountains of the Beara peninsula. The thin line of the road which connects the southern and northern shores of the peninsula is clearly visible. It winds in great serpentine loops over the summit of the Healy Pass and descends to Kenmare Bay and the towering mountains of the Iveragh peninsula.

Although the peaks of west Kerry are not

high by European standards, they soar upwards in serried ranges to culminate in the magnificent peaks of MacGillicuddy's Reeks, Ireland's highest mountains. Much of the Iveragh peninsula is a stark expanse of bare rock, raised bog and heather. Only where the mountains break are strips of forest and green fields to be glimpsed. Whilst there are quite lush belts of vegatation around Kenmare Bay and along the coast further north, the westernmost edge of the peninsula is stark and poor. Inland, the enchanted lakes of Killarney are set in a valley between the Reeks and the hilly area known as the Glens which separates Kerry from the rest of Munster. Ross Castle and Muckross House - the imposing monuments of the Medieval Gaelic Lords of the area and their Anglo-Irish successors - stand out impressively on the lakeside, whilst patches of oak forest interspersed with wild rhodedendrons cling to the valleys and lower slopes of the peaks.

North of Killarney, the Dingle Peninsula is yet more barren, dominated by the humped crest of Mount Brandon and the spine of hills that runs down its entire length. The white beach and sand dunes of Inch Strand stretch out into the sea south of the mountains, but further along the coast the impressive storm tossed rocks and cliffs of Slea Head provide some of the finest scenery in Ireland. At the tip of the peninsula the mountains break, leaving a narrow toenail of comparatively flat arable land between Dingle town and the bulk of Brandon itself. This cramped area is another repository of tradition, still Gaelic speaking but struggling to retain its identity against the tides of tourism. Thirty years ago Dingle was a small fishing port and market centre, where it was not uncommon to find flocks of sheep tethered to lampposts on Fair Day and Irish was the everyday language. Today you are more likely to hear English, German or French in its cosmopolitan restaurants and craft shops.

By now a north-flying bird would have traversed the rugged sandstone peninsulas of West Cork and Kerry. Beyond the sprawling conglomerate of Tralee, the flatter lands of north Kerry give a more placid landscape of low hills and farming country which stretches to the Shannon estuary. At this point the inhospitable Atlantic coasts break, offering a route along the great river into the green heart of Ireland. The southern shore of the estuary is hilly in places, but largely good agricultural land, its large

Traditional cottage, Crohy head, Co. Donegal.

Enjoying the sunshine, Inishowen, Co. Donegal.

At the water pump, Rathmelton, Co. Donegal.

The Giant's Causeway, Co. Antrim.

fields golden with hay or filled with well fed cattle. The signs of human habitation are much stronger, with more houses and fair-sized market towns, often clustered around some ruined castle or friary. South and east the countryside rolls into the rich farmlands of Cork and Tipperary, whilst along the shores of the estuary the mudflats provide a rich autumn feeding ground for migratory ducks and geese.

The flight of our imaginary bird now takes him over the first city he has passed on the journey, the Viking foundation of Limerick, built where the river approaches the sea. The Shannon, with its lakes and reedy expanses, is both a road inland and a wall between the east and west sides of the island. For much of its 240 mile length the countryside around turns its back on the river. The few substantial towns on its banks are found at the points where it is bridged or joined by canals from the north and east. As a highway for commerce the river is

Carrick-a-Rede, Co. Antrim.

situated on the wrong side of Ireland. Limerick, still largely a Georgian city, has declined from its heyday during the age of canals in the 18th. and 19th. centuries. Nevertheless, Shannon Airport - a few miles north - and a successful computer industry have provided new prosperity in recent years.

On the far side of Limerick, Bunratty Castle and the thatched cottages of its Folk Village stand guard over the approaches to the river and city. Further north, beyond the towering turrets of Dromoland Castle and the substantial Anglo-Norman town of Ennis, the soft green fringes of Clare soon give way to the harsher terrain of the Burren Hills. The bare limestone summits rise to about a thousand feet, a grey desert bereft of vegetation except for the unique array of flora in the soil deposits in their cracks and sheltered places. No rivers run down from the hills, for the rain that falls on them is carried through fissures to a system of underground

Hook lighthouse, Co. Wexford.

Gannets, Saltee islands, Co. Wexford.

streams which emerge lower down to fertilize patches of grassland and deciduous forest.

At the edge of the limestone plateau, where it meets the sea, flat beds of shale and sandstone have followed above the limestone to form one of the great natural spectacles of Ireland. For eight miles the Cliffs of Moher sweep and curve along the coast without interruption. A small 19th. century tower marks their highest point of nearly 670 feet from bottom to top. Away to the west of the Cliffs, the Aran Islands stretch out seawards, whilst to the north the limestone wastes of Black Head lead into the wide expanses of Galway Bay.

In an eastward direction the stony hills of north Clare slowly merge into Ireland's central plains. To the distance, over the bay, the city of Galway straddles the river Corrib as it rushes into the sea. It is too far away to make out the details of this exquisite city, but the bun-

Fishermen, Kilmore Quay, Co. Wexford.

galows and modern houses snaking on the roads that lead into the surrounding countryside mark its growth in recent years. The street plan and tall old houses in the centre are a legacy of the walled and towered Medieval city, but new buildings and developments indicate that Galway has become a booming modern metropolis.

The Corrib river rushes down to the sea from the wide waters of Lough Corrib, which with Lough Mask further north,

forms a natural frontier between west Galway and the rest of Ireland. The fabled Connemara terrain - so beloved by artists and writers - is a mixture of flat bogs and patches of more fertile land bounded by a deeply indented coastline. To the west it is Gaelic speaking and retains traces of old clachan settlements, whilst stone wall systems and a sprinkling of cottages proclaim the modern presence of man. The few larger settlements of west Galway - like the freshwater fishing town of Oughterard or the

Government buildings, Dublin city.

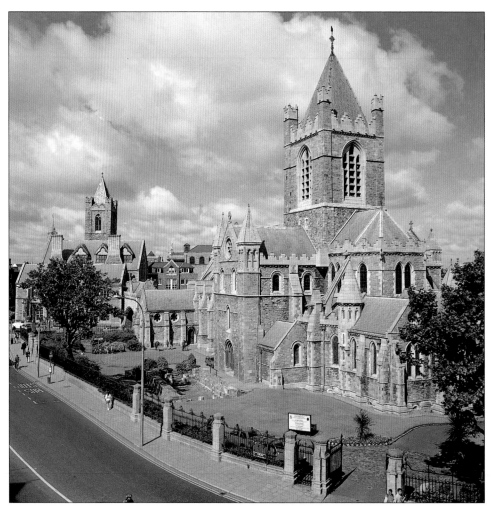

Christchurch Cathedral, Dublin city.

The River Liffey, Dublin city.

coastal village of Spiddal - show themselves here and there as a humble cluster of roofs and spires in the vast broken landscape. Further north again the scenery becomes even more impressive as the pyramidical peaks of the Twelve Bens mountains begin to dominate the horizon. In a fertile lowlying area near their southern edge, the busy tourist town of Clifden shelters besides its muddy creek, its church spires dwarfed by the surrounding peaks.

Beyond Clifden the scenery becomes wildly spectacular as the bird passes over tiny Letterfrack and enters the Connemara National Park. Small patches of forest and farmland interrupt huge expanses of bogland from which majestic peaks rise to 2000 feet. The sea has carved deep bays and into the coast and narrow glacial lakes nestle in the valleys beneath the mountains. At the foot of a cliff besides one of these loughs, a majestic white building stands proudly above a fringe of deciduous trees - the

Thomastown, Co. Kilkenny.

dream castle of Kylemore Abbey, built by a Manchester speculator for his wife. Peak after peak rears its stately head on every side. At last, a few miles beyond the deep inlet of Killary fjord, the mountains fall away into lower hills - leaving the single stark peak of Croagh Patrick to dominate the approaches to Clew Bay and Westport.

The mountain is the holiest in Ireland, and the Pilgrims Road to its summit appears as a deep scar slashed upon its raw flanks. Towards the north it looks down upon Clew Bay and its myriad of tiny islands and the dark bulk of Mayo beyond - looming mountain ranges and rocky coasts hammered by the wild Atlantic gales. The pretty little 18th. century town of Westport - designed by the great Georgian architect Wyatt - is an island of civilization amidst this wild grandeur, a gateway between the agricultural hinterland of Connaught and the inhabited strips of land stretching along the margins of the bay itself. In the

The Barrow navigation, Co. Carlow.

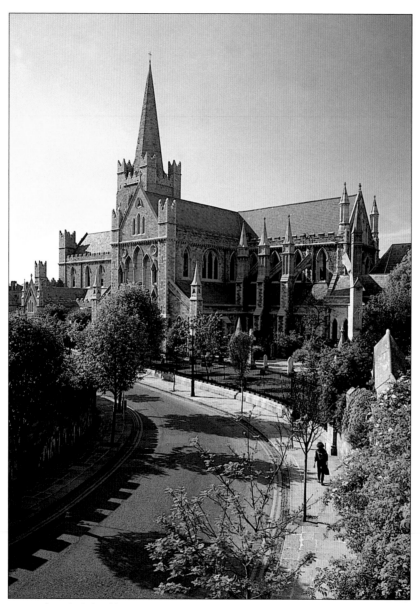

St. Patrick's Cathedral, Dublin city.

Kilkenny Castle, Kilkenny city.

16th. century this was pirate country, famous as the lair of the remarkable Grainne O'Maille, who ruled the seas around Connaught from her castle on Rockfleet Bay.

Beyond the beautiful Mullet Peninsula, Benwee Head and the cliff bound shores of north Mayo, the traces of ancient human habitation make their mark on the landscape. At the Ceide Fields on the northern coast of the County, an area of stripped away bog reveals the field walls, tombs and houses of farmers who settled the area 4500 years ago. As the bird continues along the coast into Sligo it reaches one of the cradles of prehistoric man in Ireland, the beacon-like hill of Knockarea. The great cairn on its summit - in legend the burial place of the ancient queen Maebh - is almost certainly a passage grave, whilst the remains of the largest prehistoric cemetery in Europe are nestled around Carrowmore at its feet.

Rothe house, Kilkenny city.

The bird, still flying north, would have no awareness of this bitter border, yet might notice the high observation posts which punctuate the British side. Before him, the vast granite expanse of Donegal - its quartzite peaks rising range upon range to the tip of the island - afford a view to rival any seen on his odyssey. Beyond the small town of Donegal, with its restored castle and shattered Franciscan friary, only two routes lead into the hinterland. The first road goes north-east, joining Donegal to Letterkenny at the base of Lough Swilly - leaving the bulk of the county to the west and north. The second route leads east, following the coast past the fishing village of Killybegs. Far beyond its trawlers and the armies of gulls wheeling over its processing plants the road peters out at the remote valley of Glencolmkille, near the westernmost point of the county.

Glencolmkille is the last stop on a road that leads only to the vast and intimidating Donegal coast, onto which so many

Powerscourt gardens, Co. Wicklow.

Powerscourt house, Co. Wicklow.

Avoca village, Co. Wicklow.

ships of the Spanish Armada were blown and destroyed in 1588. Twisting hill roads connect the little towns on the shore to the interior and each other, often crossing huge areas of uninhabited bog and bleak mountain passes. Ardara, Dungloe and the other settlements are separated by breathtaking scenery, the peaks rising until they culminate in the huge bulk of Errigal, nearly 2500 feet high. In the 19th. century the life of this countryside was unbelievably primitive, even by Irish standards. Today, it is still a land of white cottages and hill farms, its few wooded and arable areas almost like an oasis in the folds of the boggy mountains

At Malin Head, on the remote Inishowen peninsula, the northernmost point of the Irish mainland is reached. On either side two great inlets of the sea - Loughs Swilly and Foyle - provide shelter from the Atlantic storms. At the base of the peninsula - just across the border in Northern Ireland - the little city of Derry

Winter, Blessington lake, Co. Wicklow.

nestles within the circuit of its walls. Although the town dates from the plantation of Ulster in the 1600's, the haven on which it stands has been a northern gateway into the almost impenetrable interior since ancient times.

The bird has left the traditional bounds of the West of Ireland long behind by the time it crosses Malin Head. Even so, the stretch of coast that continues around the north east corner of Ireland is a natural extension of the region.

Geologically this part of Ulster is dominated by great flows of basalt, overlaying deposits of chalk, clays and redstone. As a result the appearance of the coast changes after Inishowen. Turning east the bird finds itself heading along a craggy dark coast past the remarkable rock castle of Dunluce, once the chief fortress of the Scottish MacDonnells who ruled this coast. Following a line of sandy beaches it eventually reaches the spectacular basalt cliffs of the so called Causeway Coast. Very soon the octago-

Autumn, Kilbride, Co. Wicklow.

Blarney castle, Blarney, Co. Cork.

Dunguaire castle, Co. Galway.

nal blocks of Ireland's most famous rock formation - the Giants Causeway - are passed. Out to sea the little island on Rathlin rides the waves like a ship. Around Fair Head warm red sandstone predominate in the sea cliffs, topped by flat moorland which preserves Neolithic settlements beneath its peat. The deserted area is an important haunt of gulls and other birds, notably raptors like the buzzard and the rare golden eagle.

The long flight around the Atlantic coast is nearly over. The last stop of our imaginary bird is the Glens of Antrim - nine deep glacial valleys facing the Mull of Kintyre. Here it might be said that the Atlantic ends and the Irish Sea begins. Before the 1830's - when the road that now sweeps around the coast was built - the Glens were isolated from the rest of Ireland by the difficult terrain of the Antrim plateau. They were in closer contact with the areas over the North Channel in Scotland than the rest of

Enniskillen castle, Co. Fermanagh.

Ulster, keeping the Gaelic language and old way of life well into the 19th. century. The waters off these shores are known as the sea of Moy. There could be no more suitable ending to a bird's journey than to recall it was on these waters that the Children of Lir spent 300 years of their exile as swans.

## DUBLIN AND THE EAST COAST

The east and south coasts of Ireland presents a very different aspect to the world than the west. For much of their length these shores are open to the interior and a series of deep bays and river estuaries offer fine harbours for shipping. This is particularly true of the shoreline facing North Wales and the north eastern part of England. From the Mourne Mountains in southern Ulster to the

White island, Lough Erne, Co. Fermanagh.

Wicklow Mountains the flat central plain reaches out to meet the sea. Two river systems - the Boyne and the Liffey - offer access to some of the best arable land in Ireland. This region has long been the most important gateway into the island from England. Its most important city, Dublin, is the capital of the country and its major cultural and economic centre.

The history of Dublin reflects the changes brought about in Ireland by the domination of England over the last 1000 years. Its beginnings date back to the Viking era, when Ireland's turbulent self contained society of little kingdoms and powerful monasteries was turned upside down by Norse invaders. They came first as pirates around A.D. 800, swooping down on coastal monasteries and sailing up the Shannon and other rivers to loot inland. Towards the middle of the century they turned from robbery to conquest, making determined efforts to establish themselves on Irish soil. Initially the Vikings failed in this

Westport house, Co. Mayo.

attempt, but after A.D. 900 a second wave of invasion succeeded in establishing a number of permanent enclaves along the eastern and southern coasts and at Limerick on the mouth of the Shannon.

These scattered Viking settlements became the first real towns in Ireland. Even today the names of many Irish ports hint at their Scandinavian origins. Waterford, for example, was originally 'Wether Fjord' - the inlet of the sheep,

referring to its major export. Wexford was 'esker fjord', the inlet by the sandbar and Arklow 'Arnkel's Meadow' after some forgotten Norse farmer. Most of these Norse towns - except the important trading city of Limerick in the west -were situated on the natural hairbrush of the Irish and Celtic seas, facing towards Viking colonies in the Isle of Man, Northern England and Western Scotland. They were part of a network which reached out westwards from Scandinavia to Iceland and beyond, and eastwards

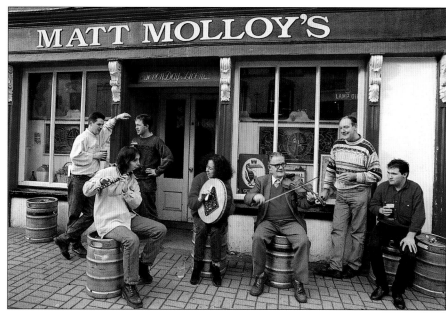

Westport, Co. Mayo.

stretched across the Baltic and led through the rivers of Russia to the Black Sea, Constantinople and the Middle East.

Dublin - 'the Black Pool' - was an important trading centre on these routes. Viking ships are believed to have used the site as a temporary camp as early as 841 and by the 900's a thriving town had grown up on the low hill between the river Liffey and present day Christchurch Cathedral. The discovery of fragments of Byzantine gold cloth and Arabic coins in Dublin suggests how far flung its connections were at the period. Its own industries included silver-working and examples of the heavy 'thistle brooches' made by its craftsmen have been unearthed in Norway and other Viking areas. The areas around the city appear to have been quite heavily settled by Norse colonists and for a time the Kingdom of Dublin became one of most powerful Viking states in the British Isles.

Tyrrellspass village, Co. Westmeath.

The Brazen Head, Dublin city.

Excavations at Wood Quay in Dublin show the Norse city to have been of wooden construction, with its small houses contained in fenced yards and open workshops lining its wooden paved streets. The city was fortified, originally with earthen ramparts, then later by a stone wall. By A.D. 1000 its inhabitants were largely Christian and in 1034 King Sitric founded the cathedral of Christchurch.

Outside of the Norse cities the Irish kingdoms changed little. Kings ruled from rock strongholds like Dunamase (Laois) and Cashel (Tipperary), whilst the great monasteries at Lismore, Clonmacnoise, Kells and elsewhere retained their great influence. Yet, inevitably, the establishment of wider contacts with the world outside opened Ireland to new influences England and the mainland of Europe. The first major developments took place in the Celtic Church, which had been corrupted by too close political ties with secular

Carrick-on-Shannon, Co. Leitrim.

H.S.S. ferry leaving Dunlaoghaire harbour, Co. Dublin.

rulers. Under the aegis of Malachy - the reforming archbishop of Armagh - the Cistercian order of monks set up an abbey at Mellifont (Louth) in 1142. The order, which followed an austere discipline based on that of the Benedictines, became very successful in Ireland. No less than 39 Cistercian monasteries were founded in Ireland from the parent house at Mellifont or English abbeys, including such important abbeys as Jerpoint (Kilkenny), Boyle (Sligo), Holy Cross (Tipperary) and Tintern Minor (Wexford). Most of these foundations were placed in remote areas away from other settlements and were self-sufficient, living off food they grew and reared on their own lands.

A few years before the arrival of the Cistercians, King Cormac MacCarthy decided to have a church built on the Rock of Cashel, which had been given to the Church in 1101. Rather than use Irish builders, he imported English masons to erect a church in the

Christmas in Grafton street, Dublin city.

Sunset, the Ha'penny bridge, Dublin city.

The Four Courts, Dublin city.

Romanesque style. Cormac's Chapel still stands and is today considered the finest 12th. century building in Ireland. Influenced by its example, an Irish version of Romanesque architecture flourished and replaced earlier styles.

The Cistercians and other orders like the Augustinians were the precursors of a new wave of invaders who would eventually destroy the old Celtic order. In 1169 Dermot MacMurrough, the exiled King of

Leinster invited Norman mercenaries from west Wales and the Bristol area to help him recover his Kingdom. The first advance party landed in Bannow Bay (Wexford) in 1169, to be followed by larger forces under the command of 'Strongbow' - the Earl of Pembroke. The Normans rapidly captured the Viking towns of Wexford and Wicklow and moved on to take Dublin, which became the centre of their activities. In 1171, Henry II, King of England brought a large

View from Killiney hill accross Killiney bay, Co. Dublin.

Sunset over the customs house, Dublin city.

army to Ireland and established his sovereigity over the island, establishing an English domination that would not be broken for over 700 years. Following his departure, Norman barons began to seize more land from the Irish chieftains, rapidly overrunning large tracts of the countryside.

Dublin became the centre of the Norman colony and its large and gloomy castle the administrative headquarters of the English Justiciar, or viceroy.

Christchurch cathedral was rebuilt by the Normans after they captured the city in 1169 and in 1190 a second cathedral - St. Patrick's - was founded just outside the town wall. The bustling medieval city, with its craft workshops and merchants houses, spread out southwards from the River Liffey. With the exception of parts of St. Audoen's church (Cornmarket) and a nearby arch and piece of the city wall, most of Medieval Dublin has been replaced by later buildings and even the Castle and its Cathedrals have been

Winter, Trinity college, Dublin city.

much rebuilt.

By 1300 the Norman colony was beginning to decline. Already Norman landowners on its frontiers were intermarrying with native ruling families and beginning to adopt Irish dress and customs. In 1315 a Scottish army under the command of Edward Bruce invaded Ireland and caused great destruction over the countryside. The destruction of towns, villages and castles badly weakened the settled areas under English rule. The Irish experienced a military resurgence and began reclaiming lands they had previously lost. The process of decay was accelerated by the effects of the Black Death around 1350 and by the end of the century much of Ireland had passed out of the control of the King's Justiciar in Dublin.

The two hundred years between 1500 and 1700 saw the end of the old Irish and Norman ruling families and their replacement by a new aristocracy of

English and Scottish landlords. By 1605 the powerful Earl of Desmond in Munster and the independent O'Neill and O'Donnell Lords of Ulster had been conquered along with many lesser chieftains. Under the Tudor and Stuart dynasties attempts were made to pacify Ireland by planting English and Scottish settlers on lands confiscated from Irish rebels. In Leinster and Munster new English landowners took over existing castles such as Lismore (Waterford) or built themselves fortified houses like Mallow (Cork) and Huntingdon (Carlow). Some Irish lords who had surrendered to the new order also built new homes, most notably Richard Burke, Earl of Clanricarde, who built a magnificent house at Portumna (Galway) in 1618.

By far the most important plantations took place in Ulster. Before the defeat in 1603 of the great rebellion led by Hugh O'Neill, the heartlands of Ulster had been the most Gaelic part of Ireland. Behind the barrier of mountains, drumlins and lakes which divided Ulster from the rest of Ireland, the life of the people had changed little in a 1000 years. However, the 'Flight of the Earls' in 1607 - which saw the leading lords of Ulster flee to Spain - led to over a half million acres of profitable land being made available for settlement.

The Ulster plantations changed the face of Ireland permanently as large areas of the province were colonized by Protestants from the lowlands of Scotland. This Protestant colony survived several rebellions by the native Irish in the 17th. century and eventually came to outnumber their Catholic neighbours in the northern part of the island. Before the settlement there were few towns or even stone buildings in Ulster. In 1624 Londonderry, the last walled city built in Europe, became one of the first and most important foundations of the Plantation. On Lough Erne in Fermanagh the Maguire castle at Enniskillen was rebuilt and became the centre of another important town. Throughout the countryside there was a flurry of building activity as fortified houses and villages were erected on confiscated lands. Some of the planters appear to have brought their own masons, since 17th. century castles like Monea (Fermanagh), Tully (Fermanagh) and Ballygally (Tyrone) have very strong Scottish features.

Dublin and the rest of Ireland have seen equally great changes since 1600. The 17th. century saw the continuation of the cycle of wars and confiscations which had been started by Henry VIII with the crushing of the Earldom of Kildare in 1534. By 1700 only one seventh of the land of Ireland remained in Catholic hands. The rest had passed to a new Protestant landowning class introduced from England and Scotland. Roman Catholics - who made up the bulk of the population - were excluded from political and economic life by a series of 'Penal Laws'. Power rested firmly in the hands of the 'Ascendancy', the descendants of the Protestant English colonists who settled in Ireland during the Tudor and Stuart eras. The Irish Parliament - which was based in Dublin - became the principal organ through which the views of this elite minority were passed onto the English government in London.

The years of peace after 1700 saw great developments in Ireland, although economic progress was blocked by English controls on exports. Landlords grew rich from the rents of their tenants or began improving their lands.

Many of the better Anglo-Irish landlords developed model villages near to or on their estates, providing better houses and amenities like schools and churches for their tenants. Sizable towns like

Mitchelstown (Cork) and Birr (Offaly) owe their foundation to their local landlords, as do the picturesque villages of Enniskerry (Wicklow), Adare (Limerick) and Tyrells Pass (Westmeath). The rebuilding of existing medieval centres gathered momentum at the same time and the towers and clay and wattle houses which were the typical domestic dwellings in Cork, Galway and elsewhere were replaced by Georgian and 19th. century town houses. Today, even moderate sized towns like Mullingar (Westmeath), Cashel (Tipperary) and Cahir (Tipperary) have some notably fine Georgian architecture on their streets.

The rural landscape of eastern and southern Ireland began to take on its present appearance in the Georgian era. The hedgerows and lines of trees which typify the field systems of the better farming regions of Leinster and Munster were laid down at this time. Better off tenant farmers began replacing their turf or clay cabins with stone farmhouses and cottages. The mass of the rural poor, living on potatoes grown on tiny patches of land, were not rehoused till much later. The land became overcrowded and it was only after the terrible devastation caused by the Great Famine and the emigration of untold thousands of

Dublin city centre.

Irish people that their lot was improved. In the late Victorian era, after 1890, a determined effort by benevolent landlords, the Congested Districts Board and Local and County Councils provided thousands of subsidized cottages for farm labourers and poor tenants who were still living in impermanent hovels.

Economic development was encouraged by the building off canal systems linking Dublin to the Shannon and other river systems. The Grand Canal - opened in 1804 - began at the Ringsend Basin in Dublin and crossed the middle of Ireland to meet the Shannon at the once busy river port of Shannon Harbour. The Royal Canal took a more northerly route from Dublin, going via Mullingar to join the river at Richmond Harbour north of Loch Ree. In the north other canals joined the Shannon to the Erne Navigation. The development of canals was matched by the upgrading and improvement of roads. Stagecoach routes made it possible for travellers to move between towns with ease. Coaching Inns like the famous Brazen Head in Dublin provided them with accommodation and food on the way. New stone bridges were built and earlier Medieval bridges like that built by the Cistercians at Abbeyleix (Laois) restored or replaced. There was also an increase in industrial activity throughout the countryside, with the erection of Linen, Woollen or Grain mills at many locations. Lighthouses were built around the dangerous coasts and harbours built or improved. In the 1800's a magnificent new harbour was provided for Dublin at nearby Kingstown (Dun Laoghaire), built with granite from the quarry at Dalkey Hill, two miles away.

Dublin expanded in the 18th. century and became a great Georgian city. A succession of architectural masterpieces - starting with the Royal Hospital (Kilmainham) in the late 17th. century - transformed the cramped and uncomfortable medieval town. Dublin Castle was rebuilt and its old Norman towers and walls demolished Nearby, the City Hall was erected between 1769 and 1779. A little distance down the road, the Irish House of Parliament (now the Bank of Ireland) began construction in 1729. Trinity College - founded in 1589 by Queen Elizabeth - was extended and its impressive Library and Front Square laid down. Leinster House, a little distance to the south, was built in 1745 and now houses the Dail, or Irish parliament.

Several important public buildings were built along the Liffey Quays, most famously the Four Courts and the Customs House, which many experts consider the finest building in Dublin. The Quays became a fashionable area, particularly around Capel Street. In addition to the many fine stone bridges which joined the older part of the city to the new streets on the northern side, the graceful cast-iron Halfpenny Bridge was opened in 1816. Like the 'Liffey heads' which adorn the city's other bridges, it has become a symbol of Dublin itself.

The terraces and squares of Georgian town-houses which are Dublin's particular glory were built from the early 18th. century onwards. The most fashionable areas were originally on the north side of the river around Mountjoy Square, the first square of Georgian houses built in Dublin. In time, however, Mountjoy and Fitzwilliam Squares and the streets in their vicinity became more popular. Eventually the Georgian terraces behind the great thoroughfare of O'Connell St.

degenerated into the slum tenements depicted in the plays of Sean O'Casey.

The centre of modern Dublin - as befits any great city - is a mixture of many architectural styles. Many important Georgian buildings are still in everyday use, like the bullet-pocked G.P.O. building or the Rotunda - Europe's first maternity hospital. The Georgian core of the city has been supplemented by later Victorian and 20th. century buildings. Some, like the beautiful little Byzantine style University Church on St. Stephen's Green built in 1855, are minor architectural masterpieces. Others, like the Bewleys Coffee Houses, date back to the Edwardian era and have a special place in the heart of Dublin's citizens. The traditional pubs of Dublin are of course rightfully famous, havens of Victorian grandeur where patrons sit at marble counters drinking the Guinness Stout which has been brewed at the St. James St. Brewery for over 200 years.

Perhaps Dublin's most famous heritage is her literary tradition. To a great extent this was laid down in the city's Anglo-Irish past, although in the 20th. century more Catholic writers have come to the fore. The first great Dublin writer was Jonathan Swift (1667-1745), the Dean of St. Patrick's Cathedral. Although mainly remembered today for 'Gulliver's Travels' some of his best writing was contained in savage attacks on English misrule in Ireland. Ireland's association with the theatre began in the later 18th. century with the playwrights Goldsmith and Sheridan. At the end of the following century Oscar Wilde and George Bernard Shaw continued this tradition in the English theatre. In Dublin the Abbey Theatre - co-founded by the great Irish poet W. B. Yeats - brought a new type of realistic drama to the stage - culminating in the plays of John Synge and Sean O'Casey. Later in the 20th. century another Dubliner, Samuel Beckett, won the Nobel Prize for 'Waiting For Godot' and other modernist plays. To this day Irish theatre is amongst the most exciting in the world, with dramatists as diverse as Brian Friel and John B. Keane still regularly producing new works.

Dublin's greatest writer was a novelist rather than a dramatist or poet. The foundations of James Joyce's reputation as one of the most important writers of the 20th. century rests on his intimate knowledge of his native city. Ulysses and his book of short stories 'Dubliners' vibrate with the atmosphere of Edwardian Dublin and uniquely recreate that lost world. Although later writers like Brendan Behan and Flann O'Brien have continued to place Dublin on the literary map, the world-wide perception of Dublin still owes much to Joyce's vision of the city.

Since Ireland received her freedom from England in 1922 she has been rediscovering and re-inventing herself. The price of modernizing the country has been the loss of much from the past that cannot be replaced. Yet public opinion slowly turned to an appreciation of buildings from the 'Big Houses' that were once despised as a symbol of unpopular landlords to the simple limewashed cottages abandoned by their owners for modern bungalows. At the same time modern Ireland - and particularly Dublin - has become far more cosmopolitan, especially since the nation joined the European Union. The restoration of the capital's derelict Temple Bar district into a cultural quarter, points towards a bright future for a new society that is moving forward whilst retaining the valuable portions of its historical legacy.

Liam Blake was born in Dublin, he is the author of several photographic books and has exhibited his photographs in solo and group exhibitions. He has won many awards including best photographic book 1985.

David Pritchard was educated at Trinity College, Dublin and now lives in South Wicklow. His published works include books on Irish postage stamps, an illustrated anthology of Irish poetry and a number of books for Real Ireland Design.

**Books in this series:**

**The Irish Pub**
**The Irish Cottage**
**The Irish Castle & Abbeys**
**Ireland**